T. S. PATTIE

Y

AS ILLUSTRATED IN THE COLLECTIONS OF THE
BRITISH LIBRARY AND THE BRITISH MUSEUM

THE BRITISH LIBRARY

BRITISH LIBRARY BOOKLETS
It is the aim of this series of booklets to introduce the British Library to the general public by drawing attention to aspects of its collections which are of interest to the layman as well as the scholar. Many of the items mentioned and illustrated in the booklets are frequently on exhibition in the British Library's exhibition galleries in the British Museum building in Great Russell Street, London, WC1.

ACKNOWLEDGEMENTS
Reproduction of subjects not in the British Library is made by courtesy of the Trustees of the British Museum.

© 1980 The British Library Board
Published by the British Library,
Great Russell Street, London, WC1B 3DG

British Library Cataloguing in Publication Data
Pattie, Thomas Smith
   Astrology
   1. Astrology
   I. Title II. British Library
   133.5 BF1708.1

ISBN 0 904654 49 4
Designed by Peter Campbell
Set in Monophoto Ehrhardt
Printed in Great Britain by
Fletcher & Son Ltd, Norwich

ASTROLOGY

Is Astrology the queen of sciences? Or is it, as the French archaeologist Jean-Antoine Letronne said in 1824, the expression of absurd fantasies, the living proof of one of those failings which have most dishonoured the human mind? No, it is rather an advanced scientific hypothesis based on the premise that the heavenly bodies give off an 'influence' which affects individual events on earth. The origin of this belief is easy to follow: the Sun gives light, heat, the seasons and the harvests, the Sun and Moon together cause the tides, and the Moon affects at least one type of mental illness, and might not unreasonably be supposed to be connected with female physiology. In the brilliant night sky of the Near East, the birthplace of astrology, where Venus is said to cast a shadow, we look up in awe at the complex and eternally recurring paths of the heavenly bodies. The further step, that each of the heavenly bodies has its proper influence on human lives, is a matter of faith.

Astrology (divination by the stars and planets, or 'judicial astrology') was not in its origins separated from astronomy (observation of the stars, or 'natural astrology'). Aristotle preferred to use the word 'astrology' rather than 'astronomy', and even in the 17th century AD astronomical and astrological tracts are bound together or printed in the same book. From the dawn of history men have observed omens of one sort or another, weather lore, the coincidence of the rising of certain stars with the seasons, and above all the phases of the moon, but in Mesopotamia they were codified at an early date. It was probably in the fifth century BC that the Babylonians, whose skill in complex calculations was a revelation to the Greeks and who knew Pythagoras's Theorem a thousand years before Pythagoras, invented the Zodiac, that division into twelve equal sections of the region straddling the 'ecliptic'. The ecliptic is the Sun's apparent path through the heavens, and it is so called because eclipses of the sun and moon can only occur on this line. The moon and the five planets Mercury, Venus, Mars, Jupiter and Saturn (which are the only ones that can be seen with the naked eye) keep pretty close to the ecliptic. It was the Babylonians again who identified the planets with certain gods, and their names, at least those of Jupiter (Marduk) and Venus (Ishtar), translated into Greek and then into Latin, are the ones we use today. People came to believe that the stars were actually gods, and it was therefore quite logical for stars to affect human lives. Even the sensible Cicero, the famous Roman lawyer and writer, could say 'Nobody can deny to the heavenly bodies the possession of reason unless he himself is destitute of reason'.

Astrology incorporated the current scientific ideas and continued to do so as it spread from Babylonia to the Greeks who secured the political mastery of the whole of the Near East and inherited its scientific tradition. By the time that the Greeks adopted astrology, the 'powers' of the planets had systematically been attributed to the stars supposed to be related to them. Astrology provided an intellectual framework for the universal science of the day by relating the heavens (the 'macrocosm') to the human body (the 'microcosm') and to stones and plants. Like the philosophy of the day, it related the four elements, hot, cold, dry, wet, to the four 'humours', melancholy, choler, blood, phlegm, and it classified bodily types by their relationships to the planets, thus 'jovial' means 'of the character of Jupiter'. Its intellectual universality made it attractive to Stoic philosophy, which dominated the Roman period. From Greek civilization astrological and astronomical ideas spread throughout Islam, from Spain to Central Asia and beyond, and mediated these ideas to

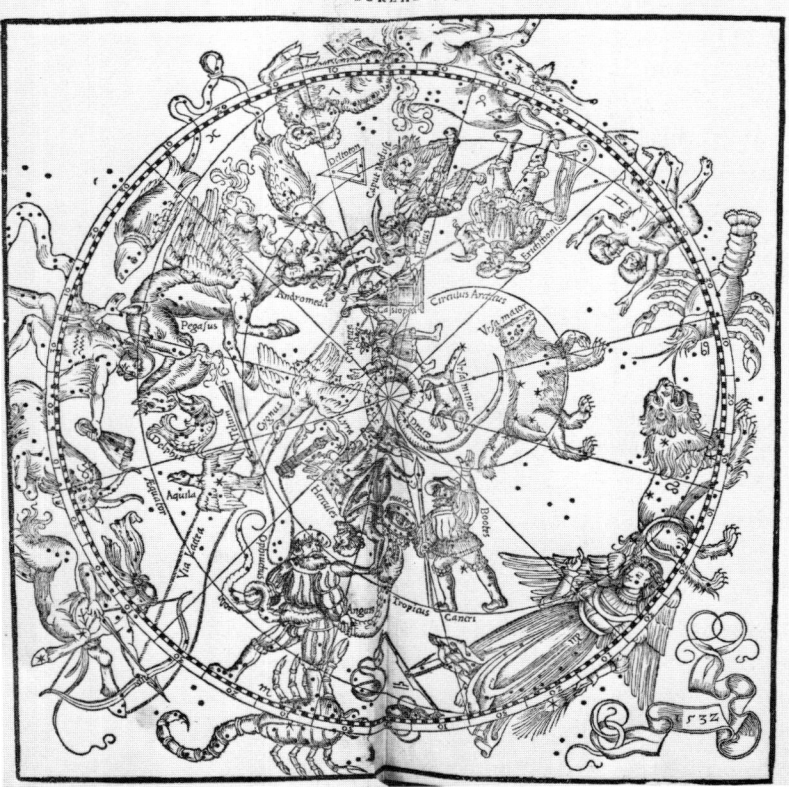

1. Northern Star map. Works of Ptolemy, *1541.* Maps C.1.c.2.(2)

Europe. It was through a Latin translation of an Arabic translation and revision that Europe learnt the works of the 'divine' Ptolemy, the great Greek astronomer and astrologer, who lived from about AD 100 to about 178.

On this foundation arose modern astronomy in the persons of Tycho Brahe and Johann Kepler both of whom supplemented their incomes by astrological predictions. Today astrology survives both in the west and in the east, as shown in the examples from India, Burma and Siam. Some Indian universities even offer advanced degree courses in astrology. Its adaptability is proven by its speedy attribution of powers and influences to the remote and insignificant planets Uranus, Neptune and Pluto which have been discovered in modern times.

THE BABYLONIAN FOUNDATIONS

The beginnings of astrology are shrouded in mystery. The earliest records come from Mesopotamia, preserved on a small number of cuneiform tablets with astronomical omens, datable to, or derived from, the Old Babylonian period (18th–17th centuries BC). These omens, taken from the appearance of the heavens, eclipses of the moon and movements of the planets, are couched in the simplest terms and the predictions are of an extremely general nature, portending little more than famine, war or peace. Nevertheless the provenance of these tablets, from Boghazkoy (in Hittite Anatolia) to Susa (in S.W. Persia) as well as from Babylonia itself, attest to the wide-spread popularity of this form of prediction. They are represented by the so-called 'Venus Tablets of Ammisaduqa', which are in fact late copies (from the library of Ashurbanipal at Nineveh, seventh century BC) of omens taken from observations of the planet Venus made in the time of Ammisaduqa, 10th king of the First Dynasty of Babylon (1646–1626 BC).

The vast majority of Mesopotamian astrological omen texts come from the royal libraries of the Assyrian kings at Nineveh, Calah (Nimrud) and Ashur (eighth–seventh centuries BC) and from the temple libraries of the principal cities of Babylon (mostly from the Persian and Seleucid periods). In these libraries the astrological omens were collected into a massive 'canonical' series of some 70 tablets, known after its opening words as *Enuma Anu Enlil*, 'When Anu and Enlil'. Although surviving tablets of the series are all comparatively late, the compilation was probably substantially complete by about 1000 BC. The first 23 tablets of the series concern omens from the movements of the moon and succeeding tablets deal with the sun, meteorological phenomena, the planets and fixed stars. The tablets excavated at Nineveh also include hundreds of reports sent

2. One of the Ammisaduqa tablets of observations of the planet Venus. Seventh-century BC copy of 17th century BC original. British Museum, Department of Western Asiatic Antiquities, K.160

by the astrologers in answer to enquiries by the Assyrian kings about such phenomena. In Assyrian times omens derived from the heavenly bodies are solely related to the king and affairs of state or public welfare; but in view of the large number of omens of other types which concern private individuals, it comes as no surprise to find that in the Persian and Seleucid periods astrological omens too are related to the fortunes of individuals.

The basic astronomical knowledge of the period was the subject of another compilation found in the royal libraries of Assyria (again probably based on much older literary tradition), the series of two or three tablets known as MUL.APIN, from the name of the first constellation it mentions, probably equivalent to our constellation Triangulum together with the star γ Andromedae. The first tablet lists the stars in three parallel 'roads' named after three of the principal gods, the 'road of Enlil', in the north, the 'road of Anu' following the equator and the 'road of Ea' in the south; it continues with a calendar of the heliacal or dawn risings of various stars and constellations and then names the stars and constellations which are setting when the first-named ones are rising. It also gives a list of the stations of the moon. The other tablets of this series are much less well preserved.

The transition from the early omens to the more exact 'science' of astrology depended on two further developments, the invention of the zodiac, that is, the use of the ecliptic as the basic frame of reference for locating the positions of the heavenly bodies, and the collection of a corpus of precise observations of astronomical movements. On present evidence the zodiac appears to have been invented towards the end of the fifth century BC. A tablet preserved in the Louvre, from the Seleucid period (after 312 BC), not only lists the signs of the zodiac but also contains a number of pseudo-horoscopic omens which assign a particular character or destiny to a child according to either a zodiacal sign, or the position of the sun, moon or planets, or the rising of certain fixed stars at the time of his birth. From at least the time of Nebuchadnezzar II (604–562 BC) records were kept at Babylon of all significant astronomical phenomena, e.g. eclipses, heliacal risings of fixed stars and conjunctions of planets. These records, today conventionally known as Astronomical Diaries, were evidently the prime source of astronomical data for Babylonian horoscopy. In addition, the remarkable growth of mathematical astronomy in the Seleucid period (after 312 BC) which is attested by tablets with detailed computations for the movements of the sun, moon and planets, allowed the Babylonians to determine with great precision the position of the heavenly bodies at any point in time, both before and after the event. This precision was achieved by advanced linear mathematical methods, with no trace of the circular and spherical geometry and trigonometry, which were Greek developments.

The skill of Babylonian scribes in manipulating large numbers is extremely impressive. Advanced scribes could deal with very large multiplication sums; in India in the early 1800s makers of calendars handled very large numbers by placing shells on the ground to represent numbers and fractions in successive sixtieths, a method that goes back ultimately to Babylonia. Although some of the Babylonian measures were as awkward as our own three feet in a yard, five and a half yards in a rod, pole or perch, four rods, poles or perches in a chain, many of them went in steps of sixty. They found it a great help in astronomical calculations if they consistently made each larger unit equal to sixty smaller units. It is to the Babylonians that we owe our sixty seconds to the minute and sixty minutes to the hour. In reality the names give away their origin – 'minutes' are 'small parts', 'seconds' are 'second parts', and we can go on subdividing into 'thirds', 'fourths' and so on. These are fractions, and whole numbers can be treated in the same way, which we call 'sexagesimal place notation'. Our own 'decimal place notation' came from India to us by way of the Arabs, and is itself a modification of the

Babylonian sexagesimal place notation. We put our units in one column, tens in the next column, hundreds in the next, and so on. In the same way the Babylonians put their units in one column, their next largest unit ('sixties') in the next column, and their next largest unit ('sixties by sixties', or 'three thousand six hundreds') in the next column. Thus our number 3767 (three thousands, seven hundreds, six tens and seven units) would have been expressed sexagesimally as 1, 2, 47 (one three thousand six hundred, two sixties and forty-seven units). The great advantage of place notation, whether decimal or sexagesimal, is that the fractions can be handled in the same way as the whole numbers. The only difficulty is to put the point in the right place.

This way of counting by sixties, in the same way as we count in tens, is called counting 'to the base sixty'. Although the idea is unfamiliar to most adults, children in school today come across the idea of using other bases, and it is particularly important because computers use the base two in their operations. The Babylonian scribe learned his tables by heart, from the two times table to the 59 times table. All 58 tables are given here in one composite table, so you can do multiplication sums to the base 60 in the Babylonian fashion. Each table, e.g. the two times table, gives all the values 1 to 20, then 30, 40 and 50. An extra step is involved in sums like 2×36: first the scribe multiplied 2 by 30 ($= 60$ or 1,0) and then he multiplied 2 by 6 ($= 12$). Then he added the two figures together, $1,0 + 12 = 1,12$. In our table the places, columns or 'digits' are separated by commas. By convention we use a semi-colon (;) to separate whole numbers from sexagesimal fractions, e.g. 2;36 means $2\frac{36}{60}$. The Babylonian scribe, however, managed without any punctuation.

THE CALENDAR

Astrology as we know it was impossible without an accurate calendar. A calendar is not as easy as it looks, as will be clear to anyone who has tried to find the date of Easter by the tables in the Prayer Book. The first calendars were exclusively lunar, that is, a new month was declared when the new moon was first seen. The interval between new moons is on average 29 days 12 hours 44 minutes 3 seconds, and 12 such intervals – lunar months – make 354 days 8 hours 48 minutes 36 seconds. How can you devise a calendar in which each month begins with the new moon and each year begins at the spring equinox? Let us say that 25 March, Lady Day, which is very close to the spring equinox, is the beginning of our year. We shall have to insert extra, or 'inter-calary' months every two or three years, either arbitrarily or in a complicated system. For example an

8-year cycle of 5 normal years of 12 lunar months and 3 leap years of 13 months (99 lunar months in all) makes an approximate agreement. It is however $1\frac{1}{2}$ days in error each cycle and apart from that it is inconvenient for the tax-collector and the accountant: even if Year 9 begins on 25 March, like Year 1, the intervening years will begin on, respectively, 14 March, 3 March, 22 March, 10 March, 29 March, 18 March and 7 March. A 19-year cycle of 12 normal years and 7 leap years of 13 months makes a much better agreement: the error is only 4 hours 28 minutes in 19 years or 1 day in 219 years. This is a better agreement than the calendar we gave up in 1752 (one day in 128 years). Our present calendar has a mean error of 26 seconds per year (3 hours in 400 years or 1 day in 3300 years), but we have stopped trying to fit in the lunar months since the time of Julius Caesar. So a calendar is really a model of the universe and similarly it is very complicated, and as it is a way of measuring time it needs a standard unit of time. Now today we can measure time in small fractions of a second, but how could we, or the Babylonians, measure time without even clockwork? Well, we should have to use the day as our basic unit. But the sun rises at different times during the year, so we cannot use the day as measured from sunrise to sunrise. Let us count the day from midday to midday, when the sun is directly overhead. This is much better, but we shall soon find that the sun does not travel at the same speed all year.

The sun travels through the sky faster in winter, as the ancients knew, so we have to take the average or 'mean solar day'. There is a further complication that you can measure the day from the passage directly overhead of a fixed star to its next passage overhead, and this period, the 'sidereal day', is about four minutes less than the 'solar day'. Similarly we can measure the year by the sun's travel from spring equinox to spring equinox (365 days 5 hours 48 minutes 46 seconds), or by the stars, giving a figure of 365 days 6 hours 9 minutes 10 seconds. It seems that it took the Babylonians many centuries of watching the heavens until by the fifth century BC they were able to make a calendar capable of projecting backwards and forwards the positions of the heavenly bodies, and of predicting the possibility of those mysterious and frightening eclipses.

The Babylonian calendar, at least as used by astronomers, was now consistent. But the Romans got their civil year (a lunar year) into such confusion that Julius Caesar fetched the astronomer Sosigenes from Alexandria to sort out the mess. Intercalary months of 22 or 23 days were supposed to be inserted every second year between 23 and 24 February (the difference between the solar year and the lunar year being nearly 11 days), but this had been done so irregularly that to correct the situation the year 46 BC (officially the

SEXAGESIMAL MULTIPLICATION TABLES

	2	3	4	5	6	7	8	9	10	11
2	4	6	8	10	12	14	16	18	20	22
3	6	9	12	15	18	21	24	27	30	33
4	8	12	16	20	24	28	32	36	40	44
5	10	15	20	25	30	35	40	45	50	55
6	12	18	24	30	36	42	48	54	1,0	1,6
7	14	21	28	35	42	49	56	1,3	1,10	1,17
8	16	24	32	40	48	56	1,4	1,12	1,20	1,28
9	18	27	36	45	54	1,3	1,12	1,21	1,30	1,39
10	20	30	40	50	1,0	1,10	1,20	1,30	1,40	1,50
11	22	33	44	55	1,6	1,17	1,28	1,39	1,50	2,1
12	24	36	48	1,0	1,12	1,24	1,36	1,48	2,0	2,12
13	26	39	52	1,5	1,18	1,31	1,44	1,57	2,10	2,23
14	28	42	56	1,10	1,24	1,38	1,52	2,6	2,20	2,34
15	30	45	1,0	1,15	1,30	1,45	2,0	2,15	2,30	2,45
16	32	48	1,4	1,20	1,36	1,52	2,8	2,24	2,40	2,56
17	34	51	1,8	1,25	1,42	1,59	2,16	2,33	2,50	3,7
18	36	54	1,12	1,30	1,48	2,6	2,24	2,42	3,0	3,18
19	38	57	1,16	1,35	1,54	2,13	2,32	2,51	3,10	3,29
20	40	1,0	1,20	1,40	2,0	2,20	2,40	3,0	3,20	3,40
21	42	1,3	1,24	1,45	2,6	2,27	2,48	3,9	3,30	3,51
22	44	1,6	1,28	1,50	2,12	2,34	2,56	3,18	3,40	4,2
23	46	1,9	1,32	1,55	2,18	2,41	3,4	3,27	3,50	4,13
24	48	1,12	1,36	2,0	2,24	2,48	3,12	3,36	4,0	4,24
25	50	1,15	1,40	2,5	2,30	2,55	3,20	3,45	4,10	4,35
26	52	1,18	1,44	2,10	2,36	3,2	3,28	3,54	4,20	4,46
27	54	1,21	1,48	2,15	2,42	3,9	3,36	4,3	4,30	4,57
28	56	1,24	1,52	2,20	2,48	3,16	3,44	4,12	4,40	5,8
29	58	1,27	1,56	2,25	2,54	3,23	3,52	4,21	4,50	5,19
30	1,0	1,30	2,0	2,30	3,0	3,30	4,0	4,30	5,0	5,30
31	1,2	1,33	2,4	2,35	3,6	3,37	4,8	4,39	5,10	5,41
32	1,4	1,36	2,8	2,40	3,12	3,44	4,16	4,48	5,20	5,52
33	1,6	1,39	2,12	2,45	3,18	3,51	4,24	4,57	5,30	6,3
34	1,8	1,42	2,16	2,50	3,24	3,58	4,32	5,6	5,40	6,14
35	1,10	1,45	2,20	2,55	3,30	4,5	4,40	5,15	5,50	6,25
36	1,12	1,48	2,24	3,0	3,36	4,12	4,48	5,24	6,0	6,36
37	1,14	1,51	2,28	3,5	3,42	4,19	4,56	5,33	6,10	6,47
38	1,16	1,54	2,32	3,10	3,48	4,26	5,4	5,42	6,20	6,58
39	1,18	1,57	2,36	3,15	3,54	4,33	5,12	5,51	6,30	7,9
40	1,20	2,0	2,40	3,20	4,0	4,40	5,20	6,0	6,40	7,20
41	1,22	2,3	2,44	3,25	4,6	4,47	5,28	6,9	6,50	7,31
42	1,24	2,6	2,48	3,30	4,12	4,54	5,36	6,18	7,0	7,42
43	1,26	2,9	2,52	3,35	4,18	5,1	5,44	6,27	7,10	7,53
44	1,28	2,12	2,56	3,40	4,24	5,8	5,52	6,36	7,20	8,4
45	1,30	2,15	3,0	3,45	4,30	5,15	6,0	6,45	7,30	8,15
46	1,32	2,18	3,4	3,50	4,36	5,22	6,8	6,54	7,40	8,26
47	1,34	2,21	3,8	3,55	4,42	5,29	6,16	7,3	7,50	8,37
48	1,36	2,24	3,12	4,0	4,48	5,36	6,24	7,12	8,0	8,48
49	1,38	2,27	3,16	4,5	4,54	5,43	6,32	7,21	8,10	8,59
50	1,40	2,30	3,20	4,10	5,0	5,50	6,40	7,30	8,20	9,10
51	1,42	2,33	3,24	4,15	5,6	5,57	6,48	7,39	8,30	9,21
52	1,44	2,36	3,28	4,20	5,12	6,4	6,56	7,48	8,40	9,32
53	1,46	2,39	3,32	4,25	5,18	6,11	7,4	7,57	8,50	9,43
54	1,48	2,42	3,36	4,30	5,24	6,18	7,12	8,6	9,0	9,54
55	1,50	2,45	3,40	4,35	5,30	6,25	7,20	8,15	9,10	10,5
56	1,52	2,48	3,44	4,40	5,36	6,32	7,28	8,24	9,20	10,16
57	1,54	2,51	3,48	4,45	5,42	6,39	7,36	8,33	9,30	10,27
58	1,56	2,54	3,52	4,50	5,48	6,46	7,44	8,42	9,40	10,38
59	1,58	2,57	3,56	4,55	5,54	6,53	7,52	8,51	9,50	10,49

SEXAGESIMAL MULTIPLICATION TABLES

	12	13	14	15	16	17	18	19	20	30	40	50
2	24	26	28	30	32	34	36	38	40	1,0	1,20	1,40
3	36	39	42	45	48	51	54	57	1,0	1,30	2,0	2,30
4	48	52	56	1,0	1,4	1,8	1,12	1,16	1,20	2,0	2,40	3,20
5	1,0	1,5	1,10	1,15	1,20	1,25	1,30	1,35	1,40	2,30	3,20	4,10
6	1,12	1,18	1,24	1,30	1,36	1,42	1,48	1,54	2,0	3,0	4,0	5,0
7	1,24	1,31	1,38	1,45	1,52	1,59	2,6	2,13	2,20	3,30	4,40	5,50
8	1,36	1,44	1,52	2,0	2,8	2,16	2,24	2,32	2,40	4,0	5,20	6,40
9	1,48	1,57	2,6	2,15	2,24	2,33	2,42	2,51	3,0	4,30	6,0	7,30
10	2,0	2,10	2,20	2,30	2,40	2,50	3,0	3,10	3,20	5,0	6,40	8,20
11	2,12	2,23	2,34	2,45	2,56	3,7	3,18	3,29	3,40	5,30	7,20	9,10
12	2,24	2,36	2,48	3,0	3,12	3,24	3,36	3,48	4,0	6,0	8,0	10,0
13	2,36	2,49	3,2	3,15	3,28	3,41	3,54	4,7	4,20	6,30	8,40	10,50
14	2,48	3,2	3,16	3,30	3,44	3,58	4,12	4,26	4,40	7,0	9,20	11,40
15	3,0	3,15	3,30	3,45	4,0	4,15	4,30	4,45	5,0	7,30	10,0	12,30
16	3,12	3,28	3,44	4,0	4,16	4,32	4,48	5,4	5,20	8,0	10,40	13,20
17	3,24	3,41	3,58	4,15	4,32	4,49	5,6	5,23	5,40	8,30	11,20	14,10
18	3,36	3,54	4,12	4,30	4,48	5,6	5,24	5,42	6,0	9,0	12,0	15,0
19	3,48	4,7	4,26	4,45	5,4	5,23	5,42	6,1	6,20	9,30	12,40	15,50
20	4,0	4,20	4,40	5,0	5,20	5,40	6,0	6,20	6,40	10,0	13,20	16,40
21	4,12	4,33	4,54	5,15	5,36	5,57	6,18	6,39	7,0	10,30	14,0	17,30
22	4,24	4,46	5,8	5,30	5,52	6,14	6,36	6,58	7,20	11,0	14,40	18,20
23	4,36	4,59	5,22	5,45	6,8	6,31	6,54	7,17	7,40	11,30	15,20	19,10
24	4,48	5,12	5,36	6,0	6,24	6,48	7,12	7,36	8,0	12,0	16,0	20,0
25	5,0	5,25	5,50	6,15	6,40	7,5	7,30	7,55	8,20	12,30	16,40	20,50
26	5,12	5,38	6,4	6,30	6,56	7,22	7,48	8,14	8,40	13,0	17,20	21,40
27	5,24	5,51	6,18	6,45	7,12	7,39	8,6	8,33	9,0	13,30	18,0	22,30
28	5,36	6,4	6,32	7,0	7,28	7,56	8,24	8,52	9,20	14,0	18,40	23,20
29	5,48	6,17	6,46	7,15	7,44	8,13	8,42	9,11	9,40	14,30	19,20	24,10
30	6,0	6,30	7,0	7,30	8,0	8,30	9,0	9,30	10,0	15,0	20,0	25,0
31	6,12	6,43	7,14	7,45	8,16	8,47	9,18	9,49	10,20	15,30	20,40	25,50
32	6,24	6,56	7,28	8,0	8,32	9,4	9,36	10,8	10,40	16,0	21,20	26,40
33	6,36	7,9	7,42	8,15	8,48	9,21	9,54	10,27	11,0	16,30	22,0	27,30
34	6,48	7,22	7,56	8,30	9,4	9,38	10,12	10,46	11,20	17,0	22,40	28,20
35	7,0	7,35	8,10	8,45	9,20	9,55	10,30	11,5	11,40	17,30	23,20	29,10
36	7,12	7,48	8,24	9,0	9,36	10,12	10,48	11,24	12,0	18,0	24,0	30,0
37	7,24	8,1	8,38	9,15	9,52	10,29	11,6	11,43	12,20	18,30	24,40	30,50
38	7,36	8,14	8,52	9,30	10,8	10,46	11,24	12,2	12,40	19,0	25,20	31,40
39	7,48	8,27	9,6	9,45	10,24	11,3	11,42	12,21	13,0	19,30	26,0	32,30
40	8,0	8,40	9,20	10,0	10,40	11,20	12,0	12,40	13,20	20,0	26,40	33,20
41	8,12	8,53	9,34	10,15	10,56	11,37	12,18	12,59	13,40	20,30	27,20	34,10
42	8,24	9,6	9,48	10,30	11,12	11,54	12,36	13,18	14,0	21,0	28,0	35,0
43	8,36	9,19	10,2	10,45	11,28	12,11	12,54	13,37	14,20	21,30	28,40	35,50
44	8,48	9,32	10,16	11,0	11,44	12,28	13,12	13,56	14,40	22,0	29,20	36,40
45	9,0	9,45	10,30	11,15	12,0	12,45	13,30	14,15	15,0	22,30	30,0	37,30
46	9,12	9,58	10,44	11,30	12,16	13,2	13,48	14,34	15,20	23,0	30,40	38,20
47	9,24	10,11	10,58	11,45	12,32	13,19	14,6	14,53	15,40	23,30	31,20	39,10
48	9,36	10,24	11,12	12,0	12,48	13,36	14,24	15,12	16,0	24,0	32,0	40,0
49	9,48	10,37	11,26	12,15	13,4	13,53	14,42	15,31	16,20	24,30	32,40	40,50
50	10,0	10,50	11,40	12,30	13,20	14,10	15,0	15,50	16,40	25,0	33,20	41,40
51	10,12	11,3	11,54	12,45	13,36	14,27	15,18	16,9	17,0	25,30	34,0	42,30
52	10,24	11,16	12,8	13,0	13,52	14,44	15,36	16,28	17,20	26,0	34,40	43,20
53	10,36	11,29	12,22	13,15	14,8	15,1	15,54	16,47	17,40	26,30	35,20	44,10
54	10,48	11,42	12,36	13,30	14,24	15,18	16,12	17,6	18,0	27,0	36,0	45,0
55	11,0	11,55	12,50	13,45	14,40	15,35	16,30	17,25	18,20	27,30	36,40	45,50
56	11,12	12,8	13,4	14,0	14,56	15,52	16,48	17,44	18,40	28,0	37,20	46,40
57	11,24	12,21	13,18	14,15	15,12	16,9	17,6	18,3	19,0	28,30	38,0	47,30
58	11,36	12,34	13,32	14,30	15,28	16,26	17,24	18,22	19,20	29,0	38,40	48,20
59	11,48	12,47	13,46	14,45	15,44	16,43	17,42	18,41	19,40	29,30	39,20	49,10

year was known as the year in which the consuls were Julius Caesar for the third time and Lepidus) was made to consist of 15 months or 445 days. In the new system a leap day was to be inserted every fourth year after 23 February, where the leap month had traditionally been inserted. To begin with this was actually done every third year and very soon another correction was needed: three successive years which ought to have been leap were not (probably the years 5 BC, 1 BC and AD 4), and the system recovered with leap years at AD 8 and every fourth year thereafter. This is the Julian calendar which lasted in England until 1752. By that time the calendar was out of phase with the sun by 11 days so that midsummer day fell on 11 June instead of 22 June. It was decided to follow the example of the more enlightened countries of Europe in adopting the Gregorian calendar. Consequently in 1752 the 2nd of September was followed directly by the 14th of September, and after that date only those centuries divisible by 400 would be leap years. That is, 1600 and 2000 are leap years, but 1700, 1800 and 1900 are not. In England people were very upset about losing eleven days of their lives, and they rioted in the streets, shouting 'Give us back our eleven days.' It did mean that people born before 1752 had to re-calculate the date of their birthdays according to the Gregorian calendar. So Lady Susan Fox-Strangways, the niece of Charles James Fox, celebrated her ninth birthday on 1 February 1752, and her tenth birthday on 12 February 1753. The new calendar had been introduced in Roman Catholic countries in 1582 by decree of Pope Gregory XIII and there was a proposal to adopt the Gregorian calendar in England in 1584/5, but the proposal was turned down because of the fear of Popery. Perhaps in view of the riots in 1752 it was the right decision.

THE HOROSCOPE

By about 300 BC it was possible to prepare 'nativities', or diagrams of the heavens at the time of birth of kings and commoners. 'Nativity' and 'native' are in origin astrological technical terms relating to the casting of a horoscope for a particular time and person. If the birth occurred during the day the stars' positions must of course be computed from elaborate tables. The earliest horoscope we know of, written in Babylonia in cuneiform script, is now in the Ashmolean Museum in Oxford. It is astronomically datable to 410 BC. One example in the British Museum (BM 35516) was written for a child born on 6.xii.169 of the Seleucid Era (= 1 March 142 BC). It lists only the position of the sun, moon and planets at the time of the child's birth, but other examples also give predictions of character and fortunes. The latest tablet of this type is dated 20.i.243 Seleucid Era (= 16 April 69 BC). By this time the cu-

3. Papyrus horoscope for 1 April AD 81. Pap. 130 (1)

neiform script ceased to be known, and the scientific achievements of the Babylonians and the Assyrians were inherited by the Greeks in the wake of the conquests of Alexander the Great and his successors.

Very few true horoscopes have survived earlier than the first century AD, even including the cuneiform ones. Two dated respectively 71 BC and 42 BC are preserved in Latin in the second-century Roman astrological writer Vettius Valens, who tells us that they came from the collection of Balbillus, the astrologer of Nero and Vespasian. Balbillus was so famous that annual games were instituted in his honour. Another early horoscope is quite extraordinary. It is a huge stone relief of a lion covered with stars, with the three planets Jupiter, Mercury and Mars above the lion's back, and a crescent moon on the lion's chest. This was part of the tomb of King Antiochus I of Commagene on the summit of the Nimrud Dagh, about 7000 feet above sea level in the Taurus range. The horoscope fits 7 July 62 BC, the date of Antiochus's coronation.

In the British Library there are several Greek horoscopes on papyrus of various dates (e.g. Pap. 110, 1278, 1526v, 2397v). Two others are much more elaborate. Papyrus 130, a horoscope calculated for 1 April AD 81 in Egypt, was compiled by Titus Pitenius at Hermopolis 'where the horizon has the ratio 7:5'. This is the usual way of expressing geographical latitude, which is in this case about

30° N. It refers to the ratio of the longest day to the shortest day, which is directly related to geographical latitude. Titus Pitenius says in a prefatory letter to Hermon: 'The ancient Egyptians, who studied the heavenly bodies and perceived that the motion of the seven gods [i.e. Sun, moon and planets] includes and directs all things, have generously left us their knowledge by means of perpetual tables; from them I have accurately calculated each god and have arranged them by degree and fraction, by aspect and phase, etc. In this way the method of astrological prediction is made correct and unambiguous, i.e. consistent. Farewell, dear Hermon.'

The horoscope itself begins with the date: 'Time of the [equinoctial] tropic of the third year of the divine emperor Titus, 6th of the month Pharmouthi [= 1 April], at the third hour of the night; on the Kalends of April, Roman style; ancient Egyptian style, first to second day of the month Pachon'. As the emperor Titus is described as 'divine', the horoscope must have been compiled after his death and deification in September AD 81. The ancient Egyptian style ignored leap years. Each year therefore contained 365 days.

The positions are then given for the Sun, Moon, Saturn, Jupiter, Mars, Mercury, then the Horoscopos (the rising point of the ecliptic), and one or two other points of astrological importance. The longitude of Jupiter is given as 'Cancer six degrees and ten sixtieths of the third order, or one twenty one thousand six hundredth part of a degree', i.e. calculated from the perpetual tables to the third sexagesimal place, 96 degrees, 0 minutes, 0 seconds, 10 thirds. The moon's position is given thus:

'The divine and light-giving moon, waxing in crescent, was running in Taurus 13 degrees and a thousandth part of a degree; in the sign of Venus; in its own exaltation; in the terms of Mercury; in a female and solid sign; like gold; mounting the Back of Taurus; in the second decan called Aroth; its dodekatemorion was shining about the same place in Scorpio'. The tables would express 'a thousandth part of a degree' as 0° 0′ 3″ 36‴. The decans, with their Egyptian names, each covered 10° or one third of a sign: Aroth extended from Taurus 10° to Taurus 20°. The 'dodekatemorion' of a planet was a point twelve times as distant from the planet as the planet was from the beginning of the sign it was in. The Moon was in Taurus 13°; its dodekatemorion should have been 156° further advanced in the Zodiac, i.e. Libra 19°, apparently a whole sign wrong. The 'terms' are sections of the signs associated with the planets. Thus in the sign Taurus 1°–8° are the terms of Venus, 9°–14° those of Mercury, 15°–22° those of Jupiter, 23°–27° those of Saturn, 28°–30° those of Mars. It is unusual to associate the Moon with gold; usually Venus is associated with gold, and the Moon with crystal.

4. Greek and Coptic Horoscope. AD 95. Pap. 98

Another papyrus, Papyrus No. 98, is famous as the 'Old Coptic' horoscope. It has on its verso the Funeral Oration of Hyperides. The papyrus itself was purchased in Egypt in the winter of 1853/4 and formerly belonged to the collection of the Reverend Henry Stobart. On the recto of the papyrus is an elaborate Greek horoscope cast for 13 April AD 95 – at least the date fits the astronomical data best. The introduction which must have included the date is lost, and the surviving part of the papyrus begins with the positions and astrological characterizations of the planets. The horoscope proper is followed by a discussion of the periods of life, first in Greek, then in Coptic with Greek paragraph headings. Coptic, it should be explained, was the latest phase of the Egyptian language, written in Greek characters with some Egyptian signs. It is an unusually detailed horoscope, followed by long excursuses in Greek and Coptic on astrological doctrine. There are so many differences from the orthodox doctrine that we may have to assume that the astrological doctrine of this date was different from the doctrine expounded by Ptolemy and other later experts. The treatise is badly damaged and the Coptic is very obscure but we give an extract:

'Third period: Jupiter decides from year 25, month 2, day 25 until year 34, month 5, day 24 [this is in Greek; the rest is in very obscure Coptic]. If Jupiter was a hostile star on the day of the native's birth, he may neglect his wife; or else he may quarrel with her; or else his children may . . .; or it may be that he will lose some

6. Sanskrit Star Map, about 1840. Or. MS 5259, ff. 56b–57 (Facing)

5. Aratus, 'Things Appearing'. Greek, 15th century. Add MS 11866, f. 1. (See page 21)

merchandise. If there was an evil star (on the day of his birth), . . . shall suffer; he shall get no children. Time and again, evil shall follow after him.' In the next period Mars is the ruler and part of the prediction is: 'If an evil star was in the Anaphora and in a malefic aspect, a woman shall cause him shame; or else he shall be a fugitive from the age of forty-two. He shall take a wife and remain married until the age of 94. He shall witness his wife's death; or else he shall be separated from her . . .'

16

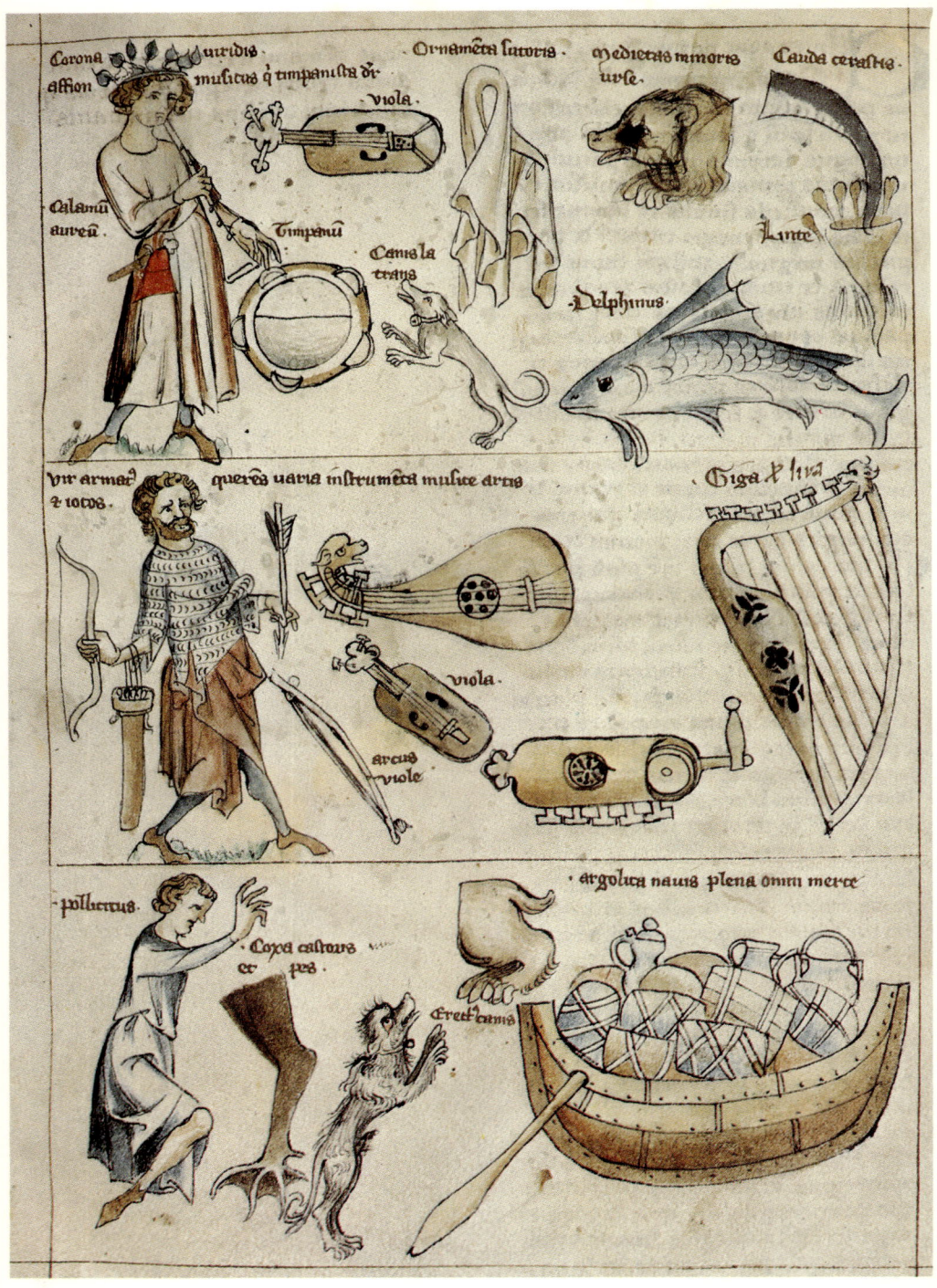

7. George Zothor Zaparus Fendulus. *14th century. Latin. Sloane MS 3983, f. 13*

8. Zodiacal Man. Guild-Book of the Barber-Surgeons of York. *15th century. Egerton MS 2572, F. 50b*

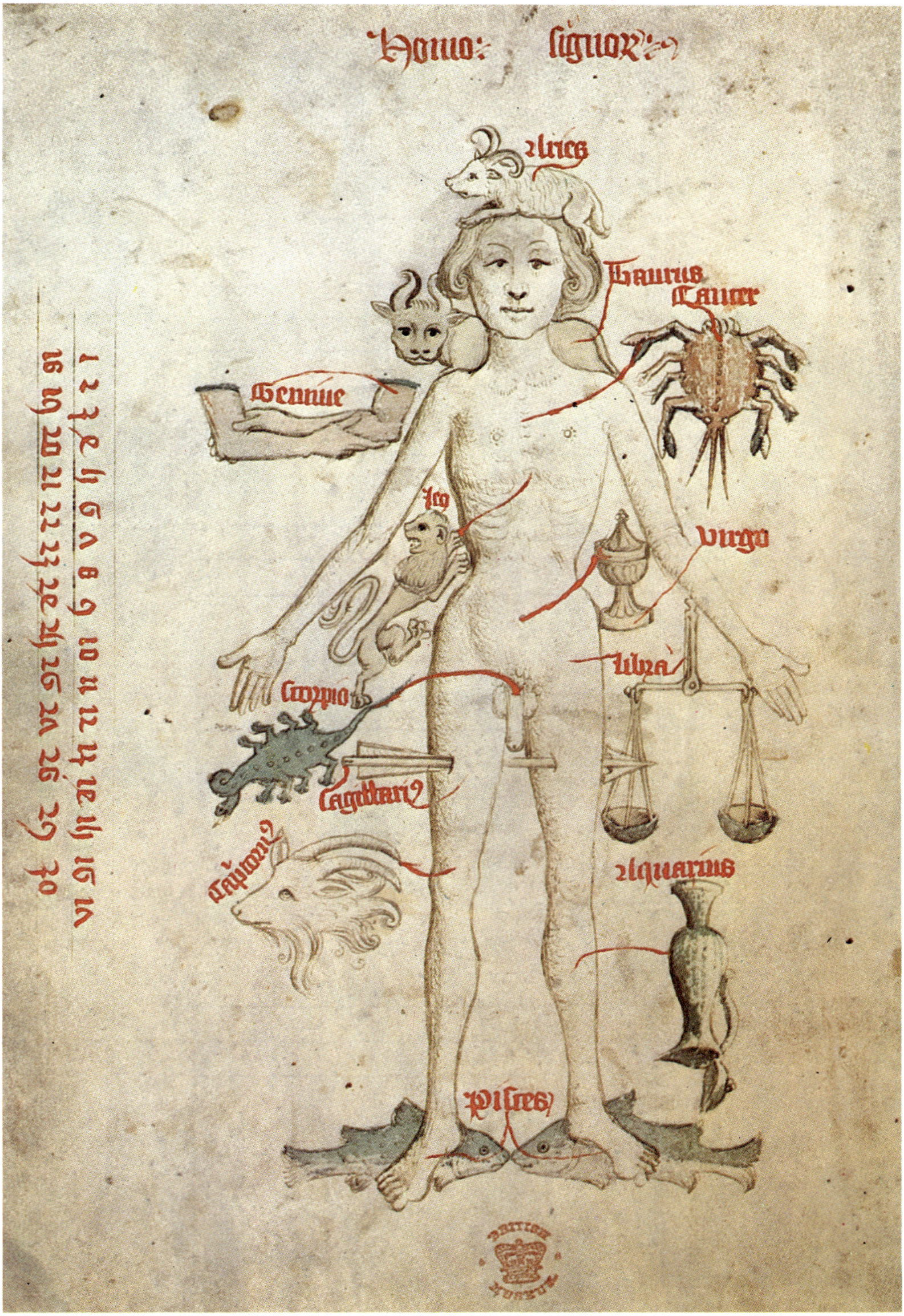

Homo signor[um]

- Aries
- Taurus
- Cancer
- Geminie
- Leo
- Virgo
- Scorpio
- Libra
- Sagittarius
- Capricornus
- Aquarius
- Pisces

9. A. *Dante and Beatrice visit the inhabitants of the circle of the moon.*
   B. *Beatrice explains some scientific theories to Dante. 15th century. Yates Thompson MS 36, ff. 131, 132*

It is clear that the two papyrus horoscopes were based on very considerable astronomical knowledge. The astronomical data of the Babylonians became available to the Greeks, who applied a totally different and fruitful mathematical theory, that of circular motion in the celestial sphere. The earliest Greek astronomer worthy of the name is Eudoxos of Cnidos, born about 408 BC who died about 355 BC. Eudoxos did not believe the stars affected human lives. He wrote a book called 'Phaenomena' or 'Things Appearing' which was used by Aratus (about 315–240/239 BC) as the basis for his poem of the same title, which he wrote at the request of Antigonos Gonatas, King of Macedonia. The poem was enormously successful despite some glaring inaccuracies and was translated into Latin several times. One Greek manuscript (Additional MS 11886) was copied in Italy in the 15th century for a member of the Medici family, whose arms appear in the border. The manuscript contains the text of Aratus's

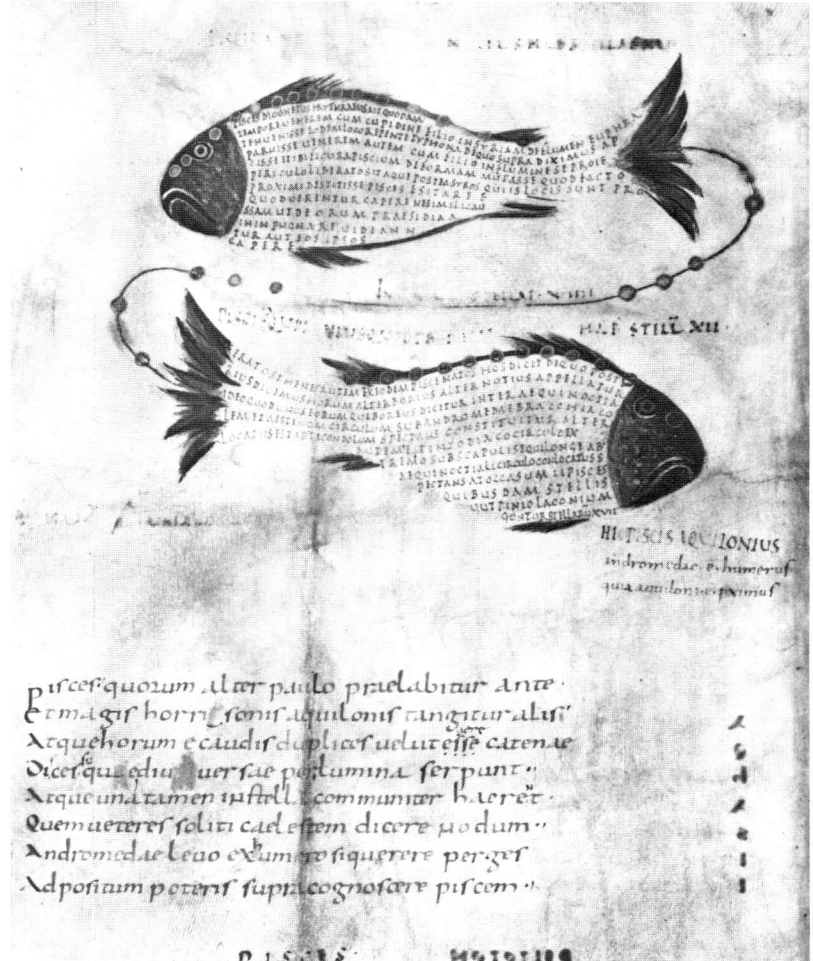

10. Pisces. Cicero's Translation of Aratus's 'Things Appearing'. Harley MS 647, f. 3b, 10th century

poem in the centre of each page with a commentary in the margin.

One of the translators of Aratus was Marcus Tullius Cicero (106–43 BC), the famous Roman lawyer and writer. A tenth-century manuscript (Harley MS 647) shows Cicero's translation in the bottom half of each page, with above it a figure of one of the constellations. Inside the outline of each figure are extracts from Hyginus's treatise on the myths of the constellations. Both the form of the drawings and the idea of shaping a text to represent an animal or object go back to the classical period.

All the works of the great mathematician and astronomer, Hipparchus of Nicaea in Bithynia, who lived in the second century BC, have been lost except his Commentary on the Phaenomena of Eudoxos and Aratus. His astronomical work is subsumed in Ptolemy's Almagest and it is now impossible to draw the line between Hipparchus's contribution and Ptolemy's. It was certainly Hipparchus who discovered the precession of the equinoxes. This is caused by the rotation of the earth's axis round the pole of the ecliptic, a yawing movement like that of a spinning top. This makes the spring equinox (from which the positions of the stars are measured) coincide with an earlier point on the Zodiac each year by about 50 seconds of arc, or 1 degree in about 71 years. Consequently the sign Aries (i.e. the first 30° of the Ecliptic starting from the spring equinox), which used to coincide with the constellation Aries, now coincides almost entirely with the preceding constellation Pisces. He also compiled a star catalogue of some 850 stars.

The 'divine Ptolemy', Claudius Ptolemaeus by name, lived apparently from about AD 100 to 178. Besides works on geography, optics and music, he wrote what became the 'Bible' of astronomy for over a thousand years, and his work on astrology had a similar preeminence. We know his 'Optics' only in a Latin translation of an Arabic translation. What we know of his life is little enough. He worked in Alexandria and he tells us himself that he made his astronomical observations between March 127 and February 141. Prefixed to a Latin manuscript (Burney MS 275) is this description of him, which probably is largely the conventional description of a philosopher. The Latin is obscure, but fortunately we also have the original Arabic.

'An emir called Albuguafe (al-Mubashir bin Fatik), in his book which he called "Collection of wise and witty sayings", said that Ptolemy was an outstanding man of science, overshadowing the rest, ingenious in the two arts, viz. geometry and astrology, who made many books, among which is this book called "Megisti", which means "the very greatest", which those who wished to turn it into Arabic have called "Almagesti". Ptolemy was born and brought up

11. *Astrolabe.
British Museum
Department of
Oriental Antiquities.
OA LXIX–15*

in Alexandria and observed the courses of the stars with instruments in the time of the emperor Hadrian and others. He built upon the observations made by Hipparchus at Rhodes. He was not one of the Egyptian kings called Ptolemy, as some think, but it was his name, as if someone were called "Chosroes" or "Caesar". He was of moderate height and pale complexion, sturdily built and with an easy gait. He had a red birthmark on his left cheek and a luxuriant black beard. Though he was gap-toothed and small-mouthed, he showed great elegance of expression and pungency of logic. He was irascible to the point of implacability. His hobbies were walking and riding. He had a small appetite and indeed often fasted. His breath was sweet and he kept a well-laundered wardrobe. He died in his 78th year.'

His Almagest or 'Great Mathematical Treatise in 13 Books' incorporates the work of Hipparchus as well as the work of the Babylonians. It describes the movement of the heavens as if the stars and planets orbited round the earth, although the notion that the earth orbited round the sun was known to the Greeks. It was known to the Indian mathematician and astronomer Aryabhata (about AD 500) and to the great Persian scientist al-Biruni (about AD 1030) who says of it that 'all appearances of an astronomical character can quite as well be explained according to this theory as to the other'. Ptolemy's treatise also gives the relevant theory and rules of geometry and spherical trigonometry, with all the necessary tables, and instructions for using the astrolabe, an instrument for observing the altitude of stars. Its modern successor is the sextant. Astrolabes are often works of art, several being exhibited in the British Museum's Islamic Gallery. One of those on exhibition was made in Spain, an

12. Ptolemy's star catalogue. Arundel MS 66, f. 45

important meeting-place of Islamic and European civilization and science. It shows the names of the signs of the Zodiac in both Arabic and Latin. The outer rims are generally numbered by fives up to 360 degrees in Arabic alphabetic numerals. In this system the first nine letters of the alphabet, in the order of the Old Semitic alphabet (e.g. Hebrew and Syriac), have the values one to nine, the next nine letters have the values ten to ninety, and the next three have the values 100, 200, 300. In the field of astronomy the Greek tradition ensured the survival of this system, apparently a Semitic invention, despite the superiority of the numerical symbols we now use, which Islam learnt from India and used in contexts outside astronomy.

Part of Ptolemy's treatise is a star catalogue, a list of 1022 stars with their zodiacal longitudes and latitudes and their magnitudes. The British Library has no manuscripts of the Greek text, but it has two Arabic translations from the Greek and one complete and two partial Latin translations from the Arabic. One of the Latin manuscripts, Arundel MS 66, was prepared in 1490, perhaps for Henry VII. The star catalogue is that of Ptolemy, as revised in Spain in the Alfonsine Tables and revised again in Oxford in 1440 for Humfrey, Duke of Gloucester. The revision consisted not of independent observation but of a constant addition to allow for the precession of the equinoxes. In this catalogue three longitudes are given for each star, the first for the time of Adam (set at 3496 BC), and the second for the time of Ptolemy, here set at AD 104, though Ptolemy himself gave a date of AD 138, and some people have thought Ptolemy's figures fitted better a date of AD 58. The third longitude is given for AD 1440 at Oxford. Ptolemy's co-ordinates were observed; the others are calculated by subtracting or adding 1 degree for each 70 years. The last columns give latitudes, North or South, magnitudes and planetary 'complexions', that is which planets govern the star in question.

The complete Latin manuscript of Ptolemy's Almagest is Burney MS 275, of the 14th century. It contains Gerard of Cremona's translation from the Arabic. It belonged to Pope Gregory XI (1370–78) and was given by Clement VII to the Duc de Berri in 1387. It is beautifully written throughout, with handsome illuminations. Sloane MS 2795, written in the late 13th century, also contains Gerard of Cremona's translation, but is far from complete.

Ptolemy's work was translated into Arabic under the sponsorship of Al-Mamon, Caliph of Baghdad 813–33, as part of the process by which the Arabs adopted Greek science and were able to make significant advances. One example of this translation is Royal MS 16 A. viii, a compendium of the Almagest by Nasir al-Din al-Tusi, very beautifully written in the 15th or 16th century. The star catalogue is

13. *Perseus: Al-Sufi, Suwar al-kawakib (Illustrated star catalogue). 14th century. Arabic. Or. MS 5323, f. 21b*

complete. Additional MS 7475 is an incomplete copy of the Almagest in Arabic, dated AH 615 = AD 1218. It is a different translation from Royal MS 16 A. viii.

Not only did the Arabs translate Ptolemy's treatises, they also commented on them and revised them. One such is the Description of the Fixed Stars (Suwar al-Kawakib) of 'Abd al-Rahman al-Sufi, who was born in AD 903 near Teheran and died in AD 986. He was the court astronomer of 'Adud al-Daula, a powerful ruler of Persia who had his court at Isfahan. This treatise is based on Ptolemy's star catalogue, with the longitudes increased by 12 degrees 42 minutes to allow for the precession of the equinoxes. The epoch of al-Sufi is AD 964, and it appears that Ptolemy's epoch was taken as AD 100, making an interval of 864 Julian years or 890 Mohammedan lunar years of 354 days. 12 degrees 42 minutes then represents a rate of precession of 1 degree in 68 solar years or 1 degree in 70 Mohammedan lunar years.

A 14th-century copy of al-Sufi's treatise is Oriental MS 5323, perhaps made near Samarkand. The illustration shows the constellation Perseus (in Arabic Barshawash) carrying the Medusa's head. Perseus is represented in duplicate, once as it appears in the heavens, and once in a mirror image as it appears on a globe. The brightest star in Perseus is the variable star Algol (the demon, i.e. Medusa's head), which according to Ptolemy has the properties of the planets Jupiter (temperately warm and wet) and Saturn (cool and dry). On the opposite page of the manuscript (not illustrated) is Auriga, the charioteer (in Arabic Mumsik al-'aynnet, the one who holds the reins). In this constellation is the bright star Capella, whose properties are those of Mars (hot and dry) and Mercury (changeably drying and moistening).

It was not only in astronomy that Islam made major advances. Trigonometry took its modern form independent of the sphere, and in 1429 the mathematician al-Kashi in his work on the circumference of the circle calculated the value of 2π correctly to 9 sexagesimal places, and converted this value to 16 decimal places. The sister-science of astrology, which had decayed in Europe, was revived under Islam, particularly by Masha'allah (Messahala in Europe), an eighth-century Jewish astrologer whose major work, an astrological world history entitled 'On Conjunctions, Religions and Peoples', has only survived in fragments, and by Abu Ma'shar Ja'far ibn Muhammad al-Balkhi, known in Europe as Albumasar. Albumasar

14. Albumasar, De magnis Conjunctionibus, 1489. Saturn in his chariot. IA 6690

15. Albumasar, Anthologia Astrologiae, 1495. IA 6756. Venus in her chariot

was born at Balkh in Khorasan on 10 August AD 786 and died on 8 March AD 886.

Abu Ma'shar in his book 'On the Great Conjunctions' analyses major conjunctions by zodiacal combinations, with effects specified by regions and by 'climates' (i.e. latitudes). He uses Persian royal astronomical tables and adopts a long-period cycle of the motion of the heavenly bodies which is supposed to fit the major events of world history. He computes the interval between occurrences of one particular conjunction, obviously from tables, as 9 years 3 days 14 hours 23 minutes 37 seconds 18 thirds 6 fourths 48 fifths (i.e. in hundred-thousandths of a second). 'On the Great Conjunctions' was translated into Latin by John of Seville, who lived about 1142. The Latin translation was printed at Augsburg 'by the diligent correction of the learned Master Johannes Angelus and the exemplary industry of Erhard Ratdolt and by the wonderful art of printing in which his excellence is renowned, formerly at Venice and now at Augsburg, 31 April 1489'. The illustration shows Saturn seated on his chariot drawn by dragons, with the signs of the Zodiac Aries, Leo and Sagittarius, which form the fiery eastern Triangle, or 'triplicity'. When Saturn is in Aries or another of the triplicity it signifies much rain, moderate cold and quarrels between kings. But if Mars provides his strength it means that the common people will quarrel with their king, all the more bitterly if Mars is in mid-heaven (its highest point in the sky). But if Saturn is retrograde it will be much less intense.

Albumasar's Anthology of Astrology is a short treatise on prognostication perhaps based on 'On the Great Conjunctions'. It was also translated by John of Seville and printed by Erhard Ratdolt in 1495 with similar woodcuts, but coloured. The illustrations in this book show the Sun, Moon and planets riding in their chariots. On the wheels of the chariots are the appropriate signs of the Zodiac: the Sun has Leo, Venus has Taurus and Libra. Sloane MS 3983, written in the 14th century, contains extracts from Albumasar's 'Introduction to Astrology', translated by George Zothor Zaparus Fendulus, who claims to have been enamoured of observing the stars, but finding the Greek manuscripts corrupt he travelled to Babylon and 'Carobolyni', where he translated the book of King Maymon and Calista of Babylon from Persian into Latin. Further travels took him to Damascus where he found many skilled in the art and where he translated the Tables of Maymon from Chaldean into Latin and emended Albumasar whose text he had in a corrupt state, and located 1029 stars which he afterwards depicted (1029 is seven more than in the fullest texts of Ptolemy's star catalogue). The manuscript is essentially an illustrated list of the 'paranatellons' or groups of stars north and south of the Zodiac that rise at the same time as each 'decan' or third of a zodiacal sign. The illustrations include single figures of the Zodiac and the Persian, Indian and Greek figures, in three registers, of the paranatellons; of the second and third decans of Sagittarius the Indian figures are the Lady sitting on a camel, the Fort, the Golden Man and the Bed. The paranatellons of the first decan and those of the second decan are badly related: you might easily guess that the Lion's head (top L.) and the Lion's body (top R.) were parts of the same constellation, but it is not so obvious that it is the same Boat that appears on the top left and the top right.

A list of about 70 bright stars going back at least to the time of Ptolemy has been discovered in an astrological treatise supposed to have been written by Hermes Trismegistus, who is identified with the Egyptian god Thoth the thrice-great. The treatise survives only in a Latin translation in Harley MS 3731 and in a French translation of part of it. It discusses the 36 divine decans, which we have already met, the 'paranatellons' or groups of stars that rise at the same time as each part of the Zodiac, and the influence on humans of each degree of the celestial globe, so that for example the 17th and 18th degrees of Pisces make fornicators and wantons.

The Roman writer Firmicus gives for the right horn of Taurus (in this case a particular star, not a degree) a fairly recognizable biography of the eunuch Eulaios, one of the regents of the young Ptolemy VI Philometor from 177 BC to 170 BC. What Firmicus says (Mathesis 8.31.3) is this: 'Whoever has his ascendant in the right horn of Taurus (i.e. the star Aldebaran) will be a great admiral and a great general, terrifying and tenacious, liberating many cities from siege. He will be an only son and will have no sons himself. Statues will be erected in his honour, but he will die after insulting a king.'

We may well hesitate to believe that everyone who has Aldebaran as his ascendant is predestined to have the same career as Eulaios, but Firmicus was convinced that the eternal and immutable stars are divine and have determined our destiny by the time of our birth. Astrology in this rigorous form has no place for individual free will or divine providence. Everything that happens on earth is strictly controlled by the stars in a purely mechanical way. Naturally therefore it was severely attacked by Christians and Muslims alike as leaving no room for God. The Church's disapproval did not stop Christians consulting astrologers, but Dante devised an entirely appropriate punishment for the sin of employing the arts of the devil. When in the Inferno he and his guide Virgil visited Guido Bonatti and the other astrologers he saw them suffering their eternal torment, condemned to plod wearily round their circle, but with their

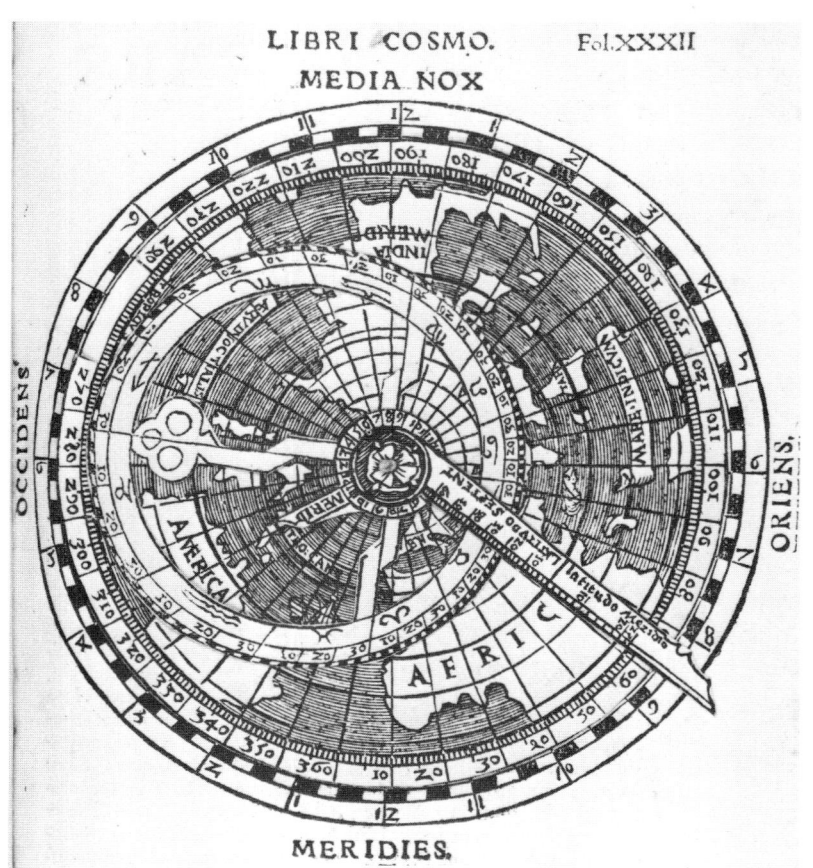

16. *Volvelles.*
Gemma Frisius's
revision of Peter
Apianus's
Cosmographia,
*1533. C.113.c.3. pl
xxxii*

heads twisted round backwards so that they were unable to see forwards. A splendid manuscript written in Italian in Siena about 1440 was illuminated by two artists. The Inferno and Purgatorio were painted by one of the artists, whose name is not known, and the Paradiso in a very different style by Giovanni di Paolo. In the Paradiso Dante is taken by Beatrice to visit the souls of the blest who inhabit each of the heavenly spheres. So we can see that Dante's picture of the world was much the same as Aristotle's, nearly two thousand years before, with the Sun, Moon and stars revolving round the Earth, each in its own sphere, with the fixed stars revolving above all the planets in a single sphere of their own.

This view of the universe sees the heavenly bodies as of the same substance as things on earth, but lighter and of course immutable. This gives a coherent picture of the whole universe, with parts of the celestial world (the macrocosm or Great World) corresponding to parts of Man (the microcosm or Little World). Each of the four elements (hot, cold, wet, dry) has its proper place in the system, as did the humours, the times for blood-letting, and the planetary 'complexions', jovial (like Jupiter), martial (like Mars), mercurial (like Mercury), venereal (like Venus), saturnine (like Saturn). It follows that doctors were interested in the relations between the stars and the human body, and incidentally it was probably better to wait for a favourable arrangement of the heavens than to purge and bleed without restraint. Zodiacal Man, a human body with the various Zodiacal signs placed in the appropriate parts of the body, is often reproduced in medical manuscripts. One illustration comes from the Guild book of the Barber-Surgeons of York, a manuscript begun in the 15th century which includes several medico-astrological treatises besides a register of the members of the Guild from 1592 to 1786.

In Europe the Renaissance saw a great revival of interest in astrology and magic, as well as more respectable disciplines. Gemma Frisius (1508–55) was a mathematician who in his 'Principles of Astronomy', published in 1530 in Latin, discussed such matters of importance to astrologers as the ascendant sign and the houses of the planets. The book has as one of its illustrations, a 'cosmographical mirror' which reproduces in diagrammatic form (rather like a graph) information extracted from tables, e.g. the time and Zodiacal sign of the rising of the Sun and Planets, and the corresponding hour at different points of the globe. Devices like these were called volvelles. They had one or more movable circles within a circle, all graduated appropriately, and were used to find rising and setting times and other matters of calendrical importance.

Dr John Dee, the Elizabethan mathematician, was interested in several aspects of astrology and the occult. He kept a diary (Sloane MS 3188 is the first volume) of his interviews with the spirits through Edward Kelley and other mediums. When he was a student at Cambridge he stage-managed the flight of the great dung beetle in Aristophanes's 'Peace'. This ingenious exploit earned him a dangerous reputation as magician. While he was at Cambridge he took 'thousands of observations (very many to the hour and minute) of the heavenly influences and operations actual in the elementall portion of the world'. He cast the horoscopes of Mary Tudor and also Princess Elizabeth before she became Queen. He was commissioned to name an auspicious day for Elizabeth's coronation, and selected 14 January 1559. He was consulted about the proposed introduction of the Gregorian calendar in 1584. Besides the newest instruments for astronomical observation, he collected several mirrors which he used to conjure up spirits. One of these is a black obsidian mirror, now in the British Museum. On the site of his house in Mortlake there now stands a block of flats called after him 'John Dee House'. He died in 1608, but his fame was so great that his name was

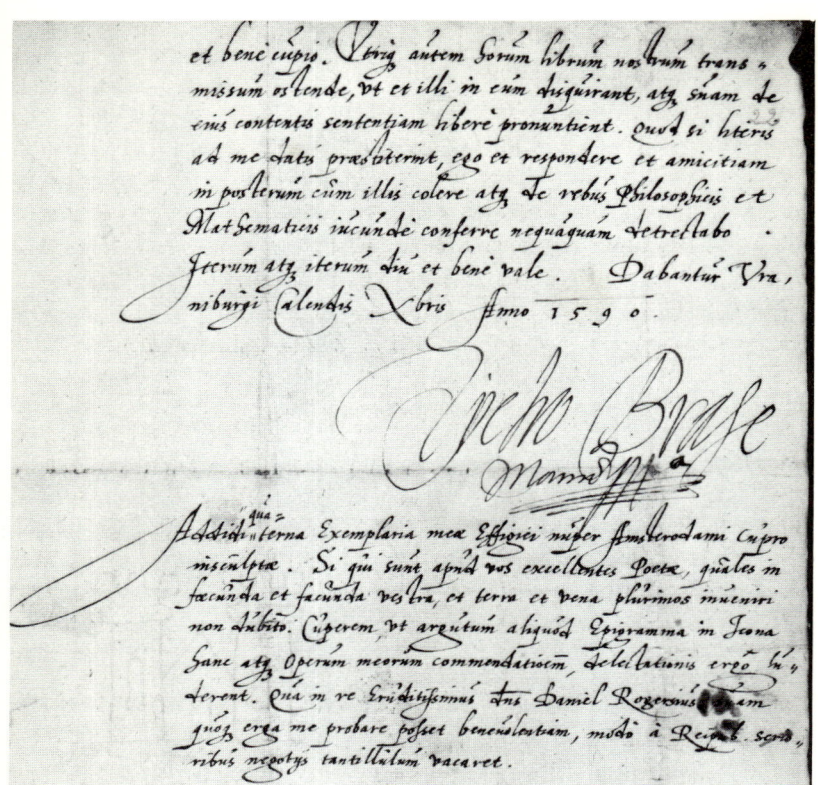

17. Letter of Tycho Brahe, 1590. Harley MS 6995, f. 22. (See page 34)

attached, rightly or wrongly, to an English treatise on the Rosicrucian Brotherhood dated 1713 (Harley MS 6485). The Rosicrucians believed that the stars and planets were directed by spirits subordinate to God, as the following extract shows. 'Behold the Rosie Crucian Crowne: This crown is set with Seaven Angels, seaven Planets, twelve signs, Seaven Rulers, Twelve Ideas, and Sixteen Figures. Observe this Harmony. The Seaven Angels guide the seaven Planets, the Seaven Planets move continually in the Signs, the Seaven Rulers run in the twelve Idaeas over the face of the Earth and with the Elements project Sixteen figures, these have their Influence upon the Seaven Mettals which you must prepare for the Diseases of mankinde, as, for Example, if Mars cause the Disease, Venus and Kedemel will cure it, and you must make the medicine of Copper. If Saturn and Zazel cause the Disease Jupiter and Hismael in Tin prepared will lend you their Influence to Cure the party. If Saturne cause the Disease, the Sun and prepared Gold will cure the Disease.' This manuscript probably comes from the circle of the Freemasons of London, who were extremely interested in the Rosicrucians at this period.

We can describe Ptolemy's picture of the heavens as one in which the heavenly bodies move in perfect circles, orbiting the Earth, and measured with reference to the Zodiac. To make the observations fit the theory of perfect circular motion, it became necessary to assume eccentrics and epicycles. As more and more observations were made, it became clear that the heavenly bodies moved in very complicated motions indeed, and Copernicus's observations required a model with far more epicycles than Ptolemy had ever imagined. Buried in Copernicus's long book is the notion that the earth revolved round the Sun, rather than the Sun round the Earth, but this is not proved in the book. It was not a new theory, of course: it was known to Aristarchus (*ca.* 280 BC) and Seleucos the Babylonian (*ca.* 180 BC). At that period it was not as successful in explaining the phenomena as the geocentric theory, but the Indian Aryabhata and the Persian al-Biruni both considered that the heliocentric theory explained the astronomical phenomena quite as well as the geocentric theory.

When Tycho Brahe, the great Danish astronomer, found that he could simplify his instruments if he measured the positions of the stars by the celestial equator instead of the Zodiac, one of the planks supporting Ptolemy's theory was knocked away. Chinese astronomers had never used the Zodiac, but always used the celestial

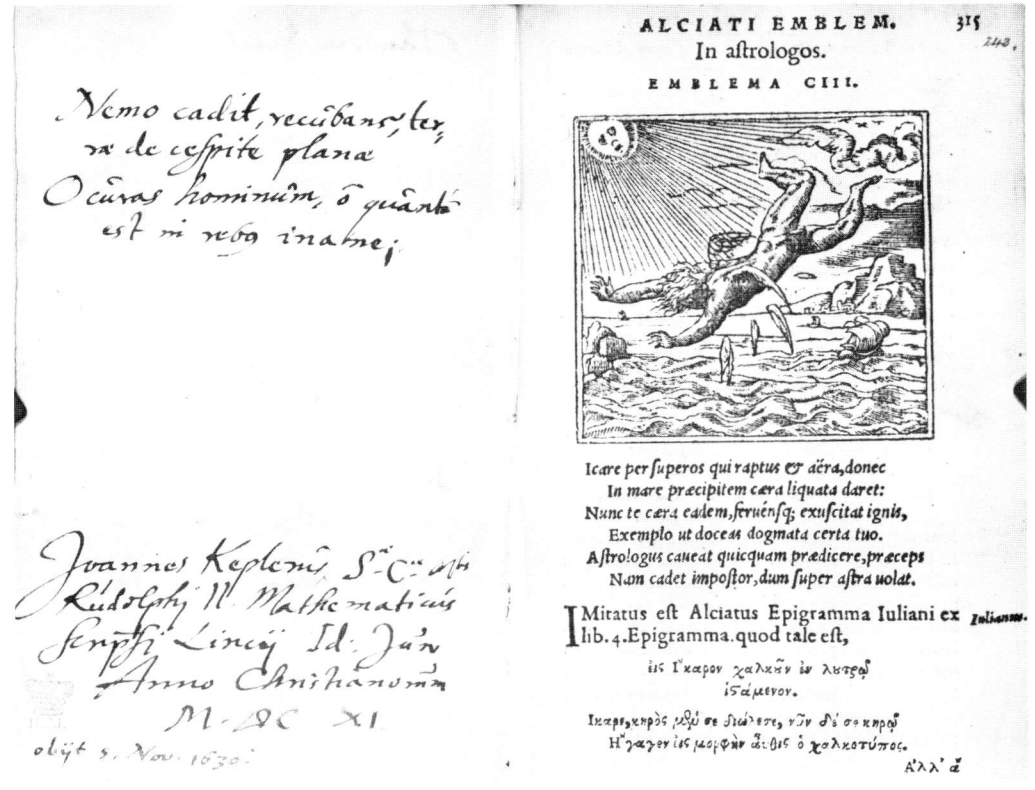

18. Autograph of Johann Kepler. Egerton MS 1234, ff. 242b–243

equator. Brahe was the first to apply a correction for the inherent error in an instrument. He conducted a prolonged series of systematic and accurate observations between 1576 and 1597 at Uraniborg, his observatory on the island of Hveen in the Sound between Copenhagen and Elsinore. In 1599 he went to Prague at the invitation of the Emperor Rudolf II, and there he was joined by Johann Kepler. While at Uraniborg Brahe kept up correspondence with other scholars throughout Europe, and one of his letters, written in Latin on 1 December 1590 to Sir Thomas Savile and accompanying two copies of his latest book, is illustrated. Kepler succeeded Brahe as Rudolf's Imperial Mathematician in 1601. He devoted most of his life to the lengthy task of preparing astronomical tables on the basis of Brahe's observations. When published in 1627 they were much superior to any tables then known. He looked for simple relations or harmonies underlying the construction of the universe. Although he began the task believing that the motions of the heavenly bodies were circular, by laborious trial and error he was forced to the conclusion that the orbits of the planets were elliptical, not circular. Both Brahe and Kepler produced astrological predictions, and Brahe was able to make capital out of the 'new star' or nova of 1572. He predicted that a prince would be born in 62 degrees North latitude, lay waste all Germany, and would not disappear for several decades. This fitted King Gustavus Adolphus of Sweden extremely well, for he was born in 1594, had a glorious military career during the Thirty Years War, and was killed in 1632 at the battle of Lützen.

Kepler composed many almanacs and horoscopes, and his horoscopes of the renowned German soldier Count Wallenstein were widely circulated. He is reported to have said 'Mother Astronomy would certainly starve if daughter Astrology did not earn the bread of both'. There is an autograph of Kepler in Francisco Sanchez of Salamanca's Commentary on Alciati's Emblems, printed at Lyons in 1573. Facing a woodcut of Icarus falling into the sea after flying too high and too near the Sun is a couplet in Kepler's hand which can

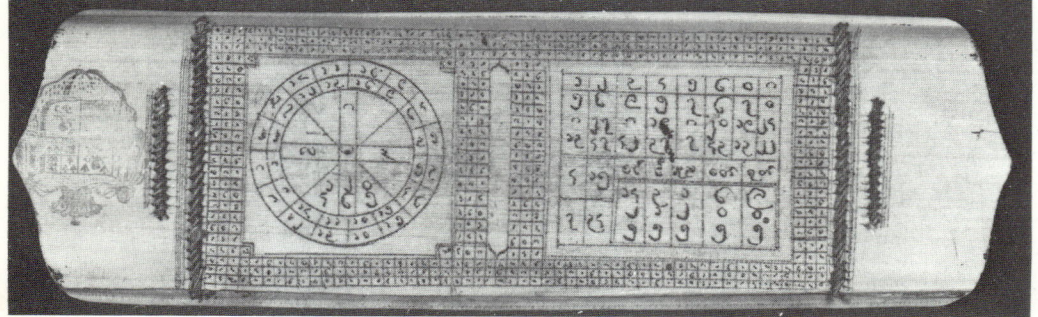

19. Burmese horoscope on palm-leaf. Egerton MS 852 C^v. (See page 36)

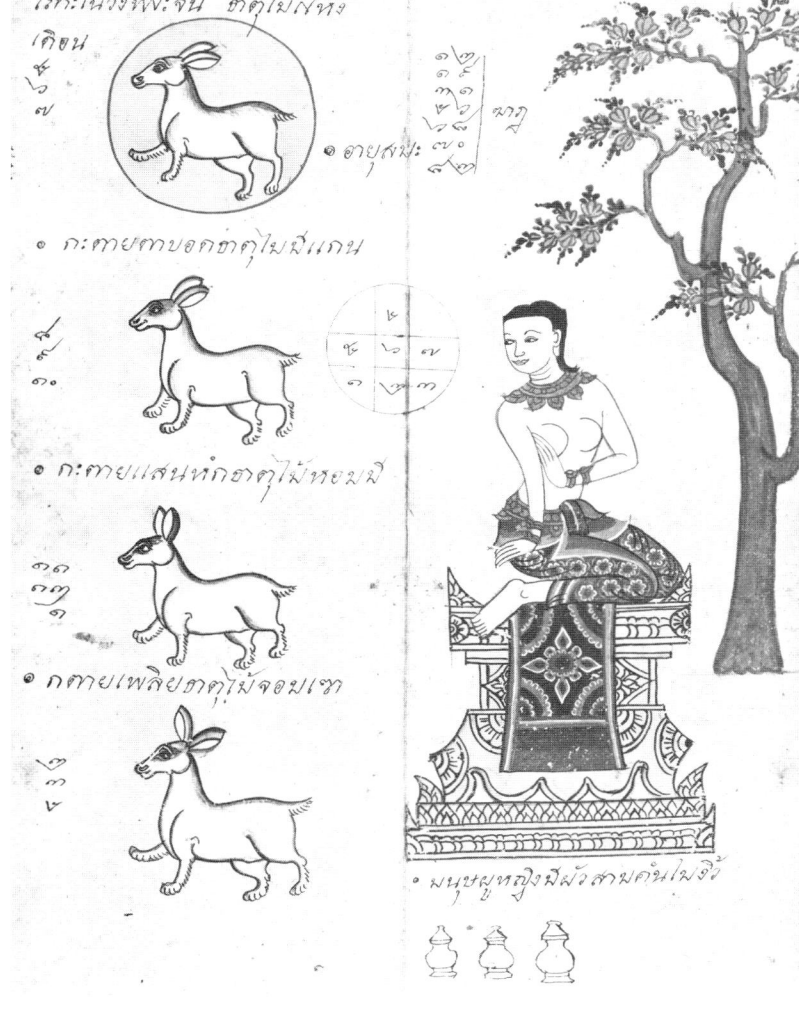

20. The hare Shashi: Thai astrological treatise. Or. MS 12167, f. 17 b-c. (See page 36)

be translated 'No-one ever fell off the ground if he was lying down already'. It is signed 'Johannes Kepler, Mathematician of Rudolf II, Linz, 13 June 1611' (Egerton MS 1234, ff. 242b–243). Kepler was one of the last to combine both astronomy and astrology. Now that the Zodiac was merely a picturesque decoration on a map and no longer the fundamental frame of reference, now that the planets were shown to move in elliptical paths and could therefore not be perfect and therefore not divine, and now that it was becoming increasingly impossible to resist the hypothesis that the earth revolved round the Sun and not the Sun round the earth, it no longer made sense to suppose that the stars affected human lives, and the beautiful correspondence between the macrocosm and the microcosm was shattered.

Or so it appeared. In 18th-century Europe the triumph of rationalism left no room for such a degenerate superstition as astrology. But the European Enlightenment did not take the whole world with it. Even in the most enlightened parts of Europe Old Moore's Almanac and its competitors kept an unbroken hold on their readers. India maintained its own astronomical and astrological traditions, enriched by Greek and Islamic science as we can see in a treatise on the Zodiac, in Sanskrit, written before AD 1840. It is entitled Sarvasiddhantatattvacudamani, or 'Jewel of the essence of all sciences', and was composed by Durgasankara Pathaka, who was born in 1787 and lived at Benares. The core of the manuscript is a horoscope (janmapattra) of Prince Navanihal Singh (1821–40) of Lahore made by order of his father Khadga Singh. A lakh (100,000) of rupees was paid for the manuscript, which contains much general information on astronomy and astrology, and a portrait of Ranjit Singh, who died in 1839. Two pages show the eastern and western hemispheres with the familiar figures of the constellations in unfamiliar costumes. The following pages show the northern and southern hemispheres. In Burma horoscopes continued to be written on palm-leaves in the traditional way, and an astrological folding book from Thailand shows no signs of western rationalism. This was written on paper made from the bark of the Khoi tree. The book is said to have been recovered from a burning temple, perhaps in Rangoon, during the Burmese War in the early 19th century. The zodiacal signs are also the animal signs used for the twelve-year cycle of the Thai and Chinese years (year of the Rat, Pig, Hare, etc.). One page shows the demon Rahu devouring the sun and thus causing an eclipse; another page shows the hare Shashi. Too small to bring any present to a visiting divinity, it sacrificed itself and the divinity translated the hare to the moon, where you can still see it.

In our own day and age we see a renewed interest in the irrational, in magic and witchcraft, and in astrology. No newspaper is complete without its column on what the stars have in store for us. The words of a popular song go 'I was born under a wandering star.' The newly discovered planets have their place in the system, though they are very distant and very small. *A priori*, astrology is no more absurd than either Chinese acupuncture or the effect of the earth's magnetism on living animals, both of which seem to work, and even though there is no satisfactory explanation of how it works, astrology undoubtedly does help some people.